SPORTS
GIRL

COMPETITIVE
BASKETBALL
FOR GIRLS

ELIZABETH GETTELMAN

the rosen publishing group's
rosen
central

Published in 2001 by The Rosen Publishing Group, Inc.
29 East 21st Street, New York, NY 10010

Library of Congress Cataloging-in-Publication Data

Gettelman, Elizabeth.
Competitive basketball for girls / by Elizabeth Gettelman. — 1st ed.
p. cm. — (Sportsgirl)
Includes bibliographical references (p.) and index.
ISBN 0-8239-3402-0 (lib. bdg.)
1. Basketball for girls. 2. Basketball for women.
I. Title. II. Series.
GV886 .G48 2001
796.323'082—dc21

2001000354

Manufactured in the United States of America

Contents

50 feet

84 feet

Forwards
They act as a link
between the rear guard
and the center, and
play both defensively
and offensively,
depending on who has
the ball.

Center
Usually the tallest player on
the team, she protects the
basket from close attacks and
takes the ball on rebounds.

Point Guards
These players control
the pace of the game
and lead
the offense.

Introduction

According to the Women's Basketball Hall of Fame, one out of three girls in America played basketball last year. This means that girls like you are out on the blacktop—with each other and with the boys. You are playing during recess, lunchtime, after school and on the weekends. You are playing with your friends, your family, and your classmates. You are playing for competition—on teams and in PE class—and you are playing for your health, for strength, for fun, and for yourself. Sports let you sweat, run, play, laugh, and learn; you challenge your body and your mind. You play because you love it.

It has been almost thirty years since U.S. courts gave girls and women equal access to sports. Title IX is a law that was passed in 1972 that says:

"No person in the United States shall, on the basis of sex, be excluded from participation in, or denied the benefits of, or be subjected to discrimination under any educational program or activity receiving federal aid."

Before Title IX, most schools refused to admit women into sports programs or had strict limits. Many schools did not have athletic programs for girls and women at all. So every time you play basketball, feel proud to be part of this important bill of rights for women.

Women's basketball has never been better or more prosperous. There is a professional league in America, the Women's National Basketball Association (WNBA), with teams in sixteen cities around the nation. College basketball is competitive and exciting at all levels—Division I, II, and III. You can play for your high school or for a club team that travels to a national tournament, or go to one of the hundreds of basketball camps throughout the United States.

For now, let's just get you started.

The Charlotte Stings's Rhonda Mapp (number 51) keeps the New York Liberty's Sue Wicks (23) away as she and the Liberty's Kym Hampton (34) reach for a loose ball during the 1999 Eastern Conference Finals game at Madison Square Garden in New York.

1

Getting into the Game

To play basketball, you need a hoop, a ball, and some sturdy shoes. Even though basketball is a team game, you can start out just playing by yourself; in fact, you should start and finish each and every day with practice, practice, practice. Practice the fundamentals, the basics of the game that will make you feel comfortable playing and make you a better and more confident player.

Before you begin, make sure your clothes are comfortable. Loose-fitting shorts, a sports bra, and high-top sneakers will set you up for a practice session without any annoying rubbing and bouncing. It is much more fun to bounce the ball than to worry about your body bouncing all around as well.

As for the hoop, all you need is anything round—your laundry hamper, a hula hoop, even a spot on a wall above your head—a target to aim at as you practice your shooting form. You might find a free hoop and a ball at the local YMCA, at your school, in parks, or at an after-school program. You can ask for a basketball as a present at the holidays or for your birthday, or ask your school if you can take one home some days—you can dribble all the way home! There are different sizes to choose from. There is a women's ball that is smaller than the standard men's basketball, because women, on average, have smaller hands. There are also youth sizes for even smaller hands.

The women's basketball is slightly smaller than the men's basketball because most women have smaller hands than men.

Rules of the Game

The goal of a basketball game is simple. The team with the most points when the ending buzzer sounds is the winner. Each team wants to make as many baskets as possible, while at the same time stopping the other team from scoring.

The Court

Basketball courts vary in size and surroundings. They can be inside or outside, with hardwood or concrete floors. In middle and high school, courts are usually 84 feet long; in college and professional teams, they are 94 feet long. The basket is ten feet above the ground and the free throw line is fifteen feet away from the backboard, while the three-point arc is twenty feet away.

The Length of a Game

A basketball game lasts anywhere from twenty-four to forty-eight minutes, depending on the level of play. Youth league games typically have four six-minute quarters. High school games are divided into four eight-minute quarters. In college, games consist of two twenty-minute halves, and in the professional leagues games are played in four twelve-minute quarters.

Playing the Game

Every game begins with a jump ball in the center of the court. The team that gets the ball is on offense; the other team is on

Basketball can be an aggressive, hard-fought game, whether you're
playing on a team or in a pick-up game of one-on-one.

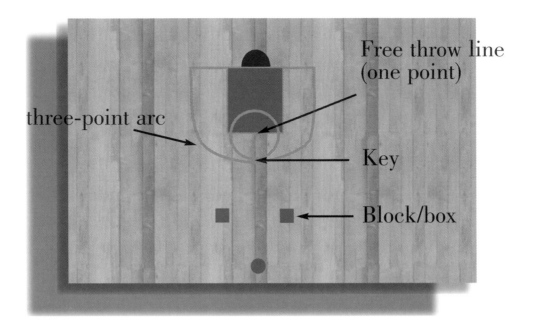

Free throw line
(one point)

three-point arc

Key

Block/box

There are five players from each team on the court during the game, and any players can go in and out an unlimited number of times during a game.

defense. The ball changes possession after a shot, made or missed, or as the result of a turnover. No player can walk or run when she has the ball without dribbling it along with her at all times. Once the player stops dribbling, she must also stop moving her feet.

Two points are scored for each basket made inside the three-point arc, three points beyond that, and one point each for free throws, which are shot after a foul. Each team defends its own basket.

A player with the ball can dribble, pass, or shoot. Each team has thirty seconds to try to score a basket. Passing to teammates allows you to then move towards the basket, cutting back and forth to get open—away from your defender—to receive a pass from your teammate.

When the Whistle Blows

Moving with the ball without dribbling is a violation called traveling. After a violation, the other team is given the ball. If a player grabs, holds, hits, or pushes another player or a referee, she is called with a flagrant foul. Each player is allowed five fouls before being disqualified. After six team fouls—when the number of personal fouls of all the team members combined adds up to six—the player who was fouled last gets to shoot free throws. If she makes the first one she gets another. This is called one-and-one. Any player fouled in the act of shooting gets to shoot two free throws. Fouls called technical fouls can also be called against a coach or the whole team for delay of game, too many time-outs, or too many players on the court. The opposing team gets two shots and the ball out-of-bounds after both flagrant and technical fouls.

The Team

There are normally twelve players on a team and one, two, or three coaches. There are ten players on the court during the game, five from each team. Any player can substitute for a teammate by checking in with the official at the scorer's table. A player can go in and out an unlimited number of times during a game.

Even though only five players from each team are on the court at one time, all team members should be in the game the entire time. The players on the sidelines can watch and learn about the other team—what shots players like to take, how well player number 32 dribbles with her left hand, and what type of plays the team runs—so that they are best prepared to enter the game themselves. They should also shout encouragement to their team.

The five players on the court are two guards, two forwards, and one center. The guards are usually the best ball handlers. They advance the ball up the court by dribbling and passing. The point guard is the floor leader—she dribbles the ball up the court and calls a play for the team to run. Usually the point guard is a fast, smaller player with great ball-handling skills. She has the ball more than any other player, although her job is to pass it to others who do more of the scoring.

The second guard, also known as the shooting guard, is a quick, accurate long-range shot. The next player is the small forward, usually taller than the guards, with an accurate outside shot and the ability to go inside and rebound. Inside, with their backs to the basket, are the other forward and the center. This second forward is the power forward. She starts from the block and posts up inside to make powerful moves to score baskets, rebound, or set screens. The center, the fifth player, is usually the tallest player on the team. She jumps center at the beginning of the game, posts up on the block, and works to block other players' shots on defense.

Breaking the Myths

Basketball has no height requirement. Dawn Staley, once a national team member, gold medal winner, star player in the WNBA, and now head of Temple University's women's basketball program, is shorter than her opponents, but she can get to the ball before anyone else. She is also fiercely determined and uses her head—her mental game—to outlast and outplay her opponents.

Guard Dawn Staley, formerly of the Richmond Rage, goes up for two points during a game against the Portland Power in Richmond, Virginia.

2 Fundamentals: Skills and Training

There are five main aspects to the game: defense, ball handling, passing, rebounding, and shooting. Good footwork is part of each of the above skills, and working on your speed and agility should be part of everything you do. Every basketball star spends hundreds of hours working on her dribble, shooting form, and defensive stance.

Basic Training Schedule

Because you're going to use your whole body during a basketball game, you must get your body ready by stretching thoroughly before and after practices and games. Work to develop your muscles, which will help you improve your skills with the ball. Train with the ball and without. Spend equal time on each if you can. If you don't have enough time in one day, then be sure to split up the drills so that you maybe do shooting and defense one day and then passing and ball handling the next. Your average training day should be forty-five minutes to an hour and a half.

- Five minutes of warm-up: Jog around the playground or around the block.

- Ten minutes of stretching: Always stretch after you get warm; this way your muscles will be warm and you can avoid injury.

- Five minutes of footwork and agility games.

- Five to ten minutes each of ball handling, rebounding, shooting, and passing games (maybe two one day and two the next).

- Five minutes of defensive slides.

- Five minutes of cooldown and stretching.

Shooting

A consistent shooter who can make shots with either hand, under pressure, and from all over the court is valuable to a team. The more you practice shooting, the better you'll be. Here are three basics:

1. Stance: Your feet should be shoulder-width apart, with your shooting foot ahead of the other foot, your toes toward the basket, and your knees bent.

2. Form: Elbows in at your sides. Make a backwards C with your shooting arm with your wrist back (like you are holding a tray). Put the ball on your fingerpads. Your other arm is the guide hand and is not used to shoot.

3. Follow-through: Arm straight up; snap your wrist toward the basket.

A good shooting stance is vital for scoring.

Practicing bank shots will improve your scoring.

Here are four games for you to practice shooting:

Snap It

Start with ten shots up in the air. Then try ten with your opposite hand. This will be difficult at first, but the more you practice the stronger your muscles will get, and the easier it will be to shoot with either hand.

Around the World

Shoot from six different spots around the court, starting on one baseline, moving to the wing, the elbow, the other elbow, other wing, and ending at the opposite baseline. Make two consecutive shots from each spot. Complete the entire trip across the court and back to make it around the world.

Bank Shots

A bank shot is made by using the backboard to make a shot. Try this: From the box, and using only your shooting hand (no guide hand), shoot until you make three out of five shots. Repeat, adding your guide hand. Then switch to the other block; repeat.

Layup Shots

Layups are shots taken on the move towards the basket. The technique used is different from any other shot in the game. From the right or left side of the basket, dribble until you are two steps from the rim. Pick up your dribble and continue one and a half steps while holding the ball (the only time when it is okay to move with the ball without dribbling). From the right side, step first with your right foot, then with your left, and shoot with your right hand as your knee comes up. Reverse this when you shoot layups from the left side. A bank shot is the best for a layup. Since layups often happen when you are going full-speed, on a fast break, or through defenders, practice different possible game situations.

Ball Handling and Dribbling

You dribble to advance the ball up the court when there is no one open to pass to or when you are not open to shoot. The more comfortable you are with the ball in your hands under any conditions, the more successful a ball handler you will be. You want to work every day to become a better ball handler and a better dribbler.

There are several types of dribbles: the crossover, between the legs, behind-the-back, spin, and speed. The more you practice all of these, the more natural they will feel. You want the ball to feel like an extension of your hand.

Three skills to remember for ball handling are:

1. Dribble with your fingerpads (your fingertips down to the first joint).

2. Dribble low (below your bent knees).

3. Keep your eyes up and look down the court.

Fingertips

Stretch your arms in front of you, palms up. Toss the ball from your left to your right hand using only the pads of your fingers. Next, move your hands down to knee level and do it again.

You must practice dribbling to be a good basketball player.

Pound the Ground

Dribble with your right hand fifty times as fast as you can, keeping the ball really close to the ground. Repeat with the left hand. Next, do fifty dribbles in front of you, back and forth from your left to your right hand with each dribble. Work your way up to 100 dribbles for each exercise.

Full Court Dribble

Dribble down the court with your right hand. Turn around and dribble back with your left. Try it walking once, then jogging, then running, and finally sprinting. Be sure to control your dribble and keep your eyes up.

Crossover

Dribble up the court, making three dribbles to the left, then cross over with one low dribble to change directions, then make three dribbles to the right. Repeat all the way down the court and back.

Between the Legs

Same as above, but this time change directions by dribbling between your legs.

Practicing the full court dribble will help you to maintain control of the ball in any situation.

23

Knowing the many dribbling and ballhandling techniques of basketball will help you be a better player.

Behind the Back

Same as above, this time changing directions with one hard dribble between your legs.

Spin Move

Cup the ball in your arm and pivot backwards and around swinging the ball back.

Once you practice each dribble separately, you can combine these moves as you dribble up and down the court.

Passing

Reasons you should make a pass include moving the ball up the court, involving teammates, and moving the defense. There are four main passes: chest pass, bounce pass, overhead pass, and baseball pass. The three skills to remember for passing are:

1. Step towards your target.

2. Aim at your target's chest.

3. End with your arms out and thumbs down toward the ground.

The chest pass is the quickest pass and goes directly from one player's chest to another's. The bounce pass skips off the ground two-thirds of the way between the passer and her target. Overhead passes travel long distances and work best when you want to pass to a teammate downcourt or on the opposite side of the court.

Following are some passing games to get you started. Whenever you pass, be sure your target is watching, and use fakes—make a move to pass one way and then quickly pass in another direction—so that the defense does not steal the ball.

Wall/Partner Pass

Practice passing the ball against a wall, or to a partner with the two of you ten feet apart: ten chest, ten bounce, ten overhead, and ten baseball passes. You can use a wall for this; just remember to aim for a chest-high target.

Pass and Shoot

Cut out from the block to the wing and receive a chest pass from your partner who is at the top of the key. Turn and square up to the basket and shoot. Repeat ten times, then switch. Practice from both the right and left sides.

Try to pass and shoot from the post, as well. As you post up on the block and your partner passes to you from the wing, make a move and shoot. Passes into the post should be bounce passes. Remember to attempt to use fakes for all passes.

Practicing "keep away" helps you learn how to control the ball and keep it out of the hands of your opponents as you pass it down the court.

Keep Away

You need three players for this game. Also known as defense in the middle, it lets you work on your ball fakes and your defense. Stand ten to fifteen feet away from another player, facing each other, with a defensive player in between the two of you. You have the ball and the defender is guarding you. You have to pass the ball to your partner without dribbling or moving and without the ball being stolen by the defender. The defender switches to the other player to play defense once

Getting the basketball on the rebound offers players the opportunity to score on a missed shot.

you have passed her the ball. Rotate positions either when the defense gets a touch or after ten passes.

Rebounding

A rebound is when a player grabs the ball after it bounces off of the rim and/or backboard on a missed shot. Rebounds are a very important part of the game. When the defense rebounds, they get possession of the ball and the other team does not score. When the offense rebounds, they get another chance to score, usually from right under the basket.

You want to grab all of the missed shots you can get. The good news is that although you do usually have to jump for rebounds, you do not have to be the highest jumper to be a great rebounder. Here are three skills that are helpful to remember.

1. Box out your player—find a player on the other team (usually the player you are guarding), turn around and make contact with your butt against their legs. Make contact by sitting down into their legs.

2. Jump to get the ball—when the ball bounces out into the court go towards it and grab the rebound.

3. Keep the ball above your chest, elbows out.

Here are some rebounding games to try.

Toss It

Toss the ball high against the backboard (or a wall). Jump to catch it—repeat fifteen times, then thirty. Once you are used to grabbing the ball off the bounce, add in an outlet pass. Keeping the ball above your head after the rebound, pivot out towards the wing and pass to an outlet player using an overhead pass.

Wonder Woman

Stand on one block facing the basket. Throw the ball to the other side of the basket by bouncing it against the middle of the backboard. Slide over to the other side of the box, then jump and rebound the ball. Then throw the ball to the other side of the basket by bouncing it off the middle of the backboard again. Slide back and catch it. Repeat for fifteen to thirty seconds.

Jump Ball

You will need two friends for this game. One player tosses the ball up in the air in the middle of the other two (not too high). The other two try to box each other out and grab the rebound out of the air. Repeat ten times and then change spots. Each player takes her turn tossing the ball.

Defense

A well-known basketball saying goes, "Offense sells tickets, defense wins games." It is true that the excitement of the game—the scoring and highlights—come on the offensive end, when your team has the opportunity to score. But good defense is the key to a team's success, and also to an individual's success as an all-around player. Defense is less a skill than a measure of heart and determination. If you practice your footwork and focus on stopping your opponent, you will be a good defender and very valuable to any team.

The point of defense is to stop the offense from scoring. This is done by stealing the ball (a pass or a dribble), rebounding a missed shot, or forcing a turnover—playing good defense so that the other team does not get a shot off in thirty seconds. Defense is played either person-to-person, where you face up and play defense against one player wherever she goes on the court, or it is played in a zone, where defenders cover a designated area of the court and guard whichever player is in their area at that time. There are three skills to remember for defense:

1. **Stay low and keep your hands up (bend your knees, bringing your thighs almost parallel to the ground).**

2. **Slide your feet, but don't touch your heels together as you move.**

3. **Keep your belly button in line with your opponent's (this way you will always be in front of her).**

Here are some defense games to play.

Slide, Slide, Slide

Practice your defensive slides up and down the court against your partner, who can practice her dribbling at the same time. Three dribbles left, then three to the right. With each change of direction, you will open up your body to the defender, keeping your belly buttons in line, with your leg dropping back and sliding along with her. Switch roles and repeat this drill.

Simone Says

One player stands in front of at least two other players. She points in different directions. When she says "Simone says slide right!" you do defensive slides to the right side of the court until "Simone says slide left!" (or "forward," or "backward"). You are out of the

Good defense keeps your opponents from scoring and is vital to a basketball team's success.

game when you stop or change directions when Simone did not tell you to. To trick you, Simone might point one way without saying "Simone says." Each player takes her turn as Simone.

Defense is a team game and help defense—where you move to guard another player or area if your teammate is having trouble containing her player—is key to good team defense. Also, taking a charge—planting your feet in front of a driving player and falling backwards on your butt when she runs into you—will give your team possession of the ball and the other team a turnover and team foul. Players that play good help defense and take charges are most valuable to their team.

Footwork Drills

These drills will help with strength and agility, and should be performed three times each week.

Plyometrics

Hop back and forth over a line, left, right, and both feet for first twenty seconds each, then thirty seconds each.

Box Jumps

Set up a sturdy wooden box, or use a bench. Jump up and down from the box, landing softly each time. Repeat ten times.

Footwork and Agility

Good footwork will help all areas of your game. Work on your speed, flexibility, and agility in each practice session. Weight lifting is another activity that you can do to build your strength. Basketball is a physical sport, with a good amount of pushing and muscling for position. Talk to your doctor and coach before starting with weights.

Nutrition and Health

When Krystal was a tenth grader, her energy was low all the time. She barely was able to make it through the day. The school trainer asked her what she ate before practice. "Chili cheese Cheetos and a Coke, that's all I have time for," she said. Krystal was not getting the right kind of energy from this junk food to fuel her through her day. The trainer suggested that she bring some leftovers from last night's dinner to have for lunch, and that she eat more vegetables and pastas. Krystal still has Cheetos and Cokes every so often, but she balances that out with healthy choices. She is now the leading scorer in her league.

Taking care of your body should also be a daily practice. That means eating right and staying away from alcohol and drugs.

3 Competition

There is a lot of talk today about winning being everything. But the top reason for playing sports given by girls and boys all over the nation is that they are fun. Yes, winning can also be fun, but kccp in mind that it is not the only reason you should play.

Teamwork

One of the most powerful parts of committing yourself to the game of basketball is becoming part of a team. Teams that work together well often have more success than teams with one or two superstars that dominate the game.

At the end of the season, only a handful of teams out of the thousands around the world end with a win. However, that does not have to mean that the season was a loss. If you can let the game

As professional basketball players know, supportive fans can be important to the success of a team.

become more a way of living—of dedicating yourself to something that pushes your limits, physically and mentally—then you can feel good about any game or season, win or lose.

Once you get involved in a school team, you will play throughout the season, usually during the winter months. During the summer, you can attend one of the many sport camps in the United States and Canada. There is a listing of camp contacts in the back of this book; for camps in your area, you can contact nearby colleges and ask if they host a girls' basketball camp in the summer. Summer is a great time to improve your skills and to work on the parts of your game that you don't feel confident about in league games.

Parents

Parents and guardians are often our biggest fans. Some may come to every game and lead cheers on the sidelines. Others may stay silent and watch intently, only to tell you on the ride home all the mistakes you made throughout the game.

Maybe there is a way for your parents to support you and show their enthusiasm in a more positive manner. Your mom could rebound for you at home when you are practicing your outside shot. Your dad could play defense when you practice your post moves. Remember that your time on the basketball court is yours.

Teamwork is necessary to succeed in the game of basketball.

4

The Future of Basketball

What do you want to accomplish in the next year? Do you want to make the varsity team? Lead the team in rebounding? Get all A's next semester? Set goals that are both realistic and challenging.

The Student Athlete

If you decide that you want to pursue basketball beyond high school, start inquiring about scholarships during your junior year. There are many colleges that offer basketball programs even if you do not get a scholarship. Research the schools that interest you and contact the coaching staff. You will then want to ask your own coach if she or he can help you put together a video that highlights your skills. Your parents may be able to help with this as well.

All basketball players in middle school, high school, and college are student athletes. Remember that you are always a student and that you need to keep learning and working towards graduation. You can never be sure when your basketball career will end due to injury, burnout, or just a desire to try something new. Getting a good, well-rounded education will allow you to keep your options open.

If you receive a scholarship and then decide when you get to school that it is too much of a commitment—you will spend well over twenty hours per week practicing and doing other basketball-related activities—have a talk with the coaches and perhaps your academic advisor.

Go For It

Whatever level of basketball you choose to pursue, you will gain valuable skills from your dedication to the sport. The strength of character that it takes to step up and dedicate yourself to a team and a sport is invaluable and will be what you carry with you each day, long after the final buzzer of your last game sounds. Whether it is basketball or another sport or passion you pursue, go for it, and play big!

Even if you only play basketball for fun, the skills you gain through teamwork will help you in your daily life.

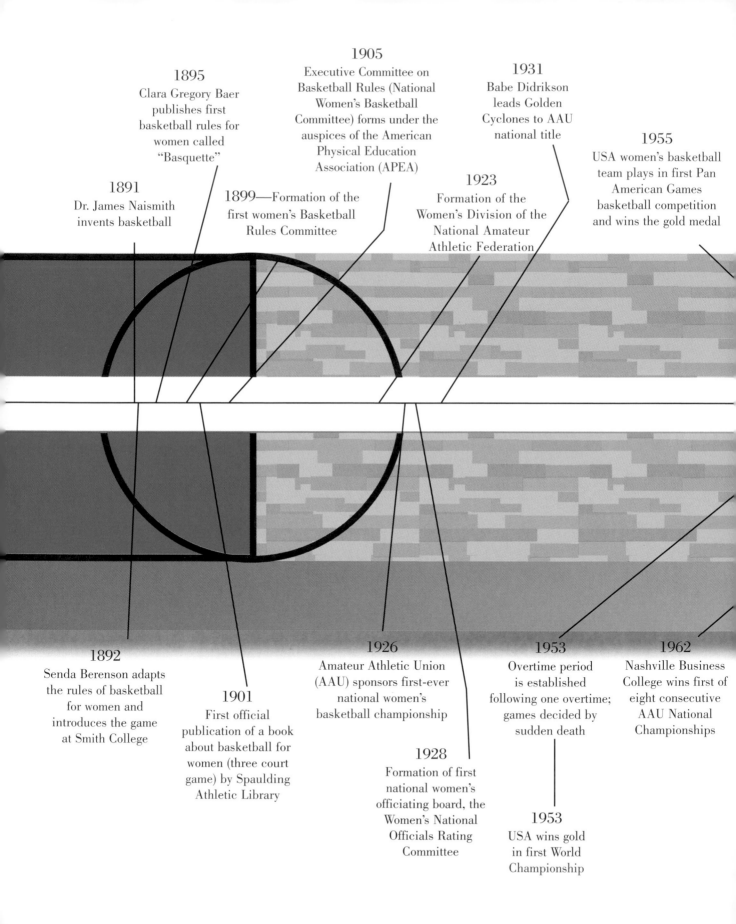

1895
Clara Gregory Baer publishes first basketball rules for women called "Basquette"

1905
Executive Committee on Basketball Rules (National Women's Basketball Committee) forms under the auspices of the American Physical Education Association (APEA)

1931
Babe Didrikson leads Golden Cyclones to AAU national title

1955
USA women's basketball team plays in first Pan American Games basketball competition and wins the gold medal

1891
Dr. James Naismith invents basketball

1899—Formation of the first women's Basketball Rules Committee

1923
Formation of the Women's Division of the National Amateur Athletic Federation

1892
Senda Berenson adapts the rules of basketball for women and introduces the game at Smith College

1901
First official publication of a book about basketball for women (three court game) by Spaulding Athletic Library

1926
Amateur Athletic Union (AAU) sponsors first-ever national women's basketball championship

1953
Overtime period is established following one overtime; games decided by sudden death

1962
Nashville Business College wins first of eight consecutive AAU National Championships

1928
Formation of first national women's officiating board, the Women's National Officials Rating Committee

1953
USA wins gold in first World Championship

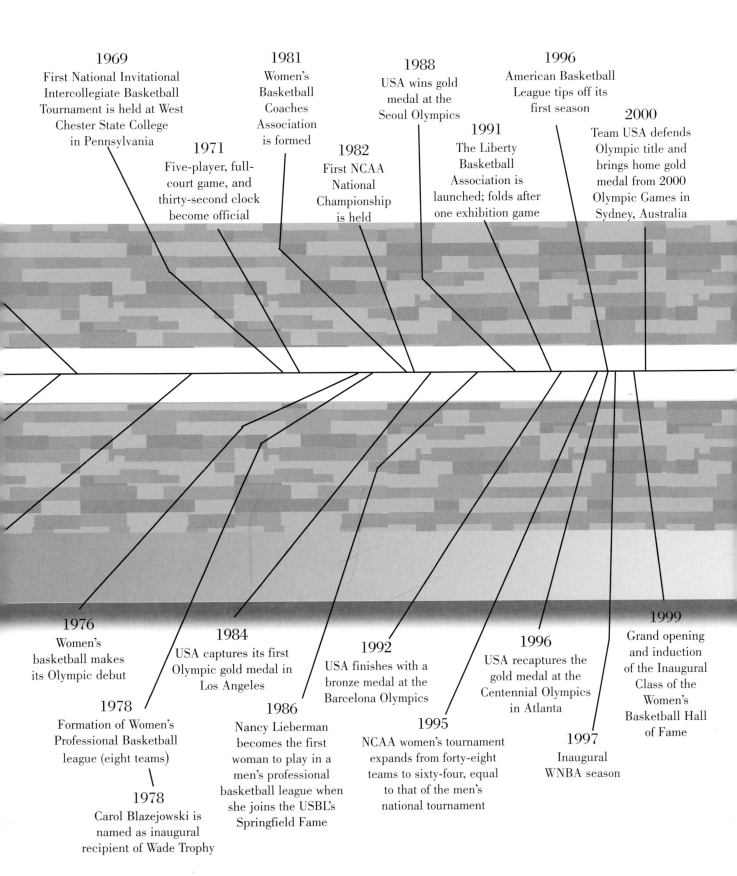

1969
First National Invitational Intercollegiate Basketball Tournament is held at West Chester State College in Pennsylvania

1971
Five-player, full-court game, and thirty-second clock become official

1981
Women's Basketball Coaches Association is formed

1982
First NCAA National Championship is held

1988
USA wins gold medal at the Seoul Olympics

1991
The Liberty Basketball Association is launched; folds after one exhibition game

1996
American Basketball League tips off its first season

2000
Team USA defends Olympic title and brings home gold medal from 2000 Olympic Games in Sydney, Australia

1976
Women's basketball makes its Olympic debut

1978
Formation of Women's Professional Basketball league (eight teams)

1978
Carol Blazejowski is named as inaugural recipient of Wade Trophy

1984
USA captures its first Olympic gold medal in Los Angeles

1986
Nancy Lieberman becomes the first woman to play in a men's professional basketball league when she joins the USBL's Springfield Fame

1992
USA finishes with a bronze medal at the Barcelona Olympics

1995
NCAA women's tournament expands from forty-eight teams to sixty-four, equal to that of the men's national tournament

1996
USA recaptures the gold medal at the Centennial Olympics in Atlanta

1997
Inaugural WNBA season

1999
Grand opening and induction of the Inaugural Class of the Women's Basketball Hall of Fame

Glossary

assist   When a player throws a good pass to a teammate that results directly in a score.

backboard   The board that holds the rim.

backcourt   When the offense advances the ball over the half-court line and then moves back over the line they are called for a violation. Also known as over-and-back.

backcourt pressure   When a defensive player guards the point guard before she crosses the half-court line.

back door   When a player fakes a move away from the basket and then cuts back behind the defense, getting a pass close to the basket for a shot.

bank shot   A successful shot that bounces off of the backboard.

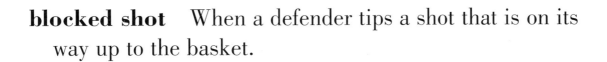

baseline   The area of the court directly under the basket and out horizontally to the sidelines. Many out-of-bound shots are taken along the baseline.

block   The rectangle on each side of the key box near the basket. This is where post players post up to get a pass and make a move.

blocked shot   When a defender tips a shot that is on its way up to the basket.

box out   When a shot goes up and a defensive player keeps her opponent behind her back by sitting back into her legs and then jumping forward for the rebound. Critical for getting rebounds.

box score   Statistics on the game that show up in the newspaper, including each player's number of shots attempted, shots made, offensive rebounds, defensive rebounds, assists, steals, turnovers, and personal fouls.

charge   When a defensive player plants her feet in front of an offensive player who then knocks her down, usually while driving to the basket. This is an offensive foul and results in possession for the defensive team.

crunch time   Usually the last two to five minutes of the game, when the game is close and every move, shot, and play is crucial.

defensive stance   Bent knees, back straight. Defense is always played low to the ground. This allows for quick moves and change of directions.

double-double   The term used when a player has a double-digit number in two of the following at the end of a game: points, rebounds, blocked shots, assists, or steals.

double dribble   When a player dribbles the ball with both hands on a single bounce, or dribbles, picks up the ball, and dribbles again without passing first.

double team   When there are two defenders guarding one player.

drive the lane   When a player drives through the key, where there are a lot of bodies, and takes a shot or passes to a teammate.

five seconds   A violation for holding the ball for too long. You have to pass, dribble, or shoot the ball within five seconds of receiving it.

flagrant foul   Also known as an intentional foul, this is when a foul is committed on purpose such as grabbing a player around the waist. Usually an intentional foul is called when a player goes after another player's body, not the ball. The offensive player gets two free throws and then her team gets the ball out-of-bounds at half court.

follow-through   The last motion at the end of a shot. The follow-through gives the ball its backwards spin and makes it more likely to go in the basket.

foul   Violation of the rules, signaled when a referee blows his or her whistle. Each player is allowed five fouls per game, six in the professional leagues.

foul out   When a player commits five personal fouls (six in the WNBA), she has fouled out and cannot play for the remainder of the game.

free throw   A shot from the horizontal line at the top of the box taken after a player is fouled in the act of shooting. Each free throw scores one point.

give-and-go   A play between two players where one player passes to the other, makes a move without the ball to get open, and then gets a pass right back.

goaltending   Blocking a shot when the ball is on its way down to the hoop in its arc.

halftime   A break halfway through the game. This is when players can rest and their coaches discuss their second-half strategy.

help defense   When a player leaves her area or assigned player and plays defense on another player in order to help her team.

huddle   When team members come together in a circle, facing each other, to talk about plays and strategy, and to support their teammates.

jump ball   Every game starts out with a jump ball at half-court. The referee will toss the ball straight up in the air between two opposing players and each player tries to tip it to her teammates for possession. If two players from opposing teams both grab the ball and claim possession the referee will blow the whistle and indicate a tie-up by raising two thumbs up in the air. In professional basketball there is another jump ball around the nearest circle on the court. In college and high school ball, there is alternating possession after each jump ball and the team whose turn it is will take it out-of-bounds.

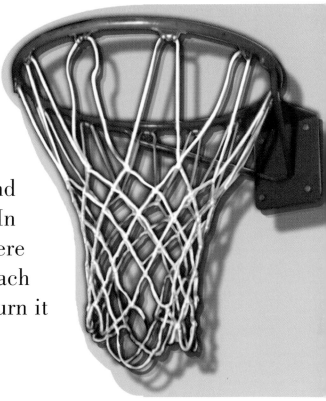

key box Rectangle that is just below the basket and extends out to the free throw line.

layup A shot made on the move, often on a fast break, after a turnover or when breaking the press. In a layup the offensive player is allowed to take one and a half steps after picking up the dribble as she approaches the basket for the shot.

off the glass Another way of saying off the backboard.

one-on-one When a player makes a move on one defender without involving teammates in the play.

on the bench The players from each team who are not on the court sit along the sidelines, on chairs or benches. They are known as bench players and can be called to substitute for one of their teammates at any time.

outlet pass Pass out from the key after a defensive rebound. Usually an overhead pass from a post player to a guard.

out-of-bounds Everything inside of the solid line around the perimeter of the basketball court is in-bounds. Everything beyond it is out-of-bounds. The ball and players are not permitted to go out-of-bounds while the game is in play.

overtime If the game is tied after four quarters or two halves, there will be an overtime period. In high school it is four minutes, in college it is five, and in the professional leagues it is twelve.

perimeter jumper A long-range shot that is taken outside of the key. Also known as an outside shot.

pick-and-roll When a player sets a screen and then pivots around, keeping the defender pinned behind her with her body. Also known as an outside shot.

pickup Basketball games where all levels and types of players come together to play. Usually played at a high pace with more offense than defense. You can find pickup games in your area by calling local YMCAs, college recreational centers, and health clubs.

player-to-player defense Type of defense, formerly called man-to-man, where each player matches up with an opponent and guards her.

point guard The position of the player who dribbles the ball up the court and calls the plays.

post-up When a player turns her back to the basket, usually on the block, keeps her defender on her back by bending her knees and sitting back into the defense, and holds her hands up for an entry pass.

press When a team plays defense full-court.

rebound When the offense or defense grabs a missed shot after it bounces off the rim and/or backboard.

screen When an offensive player blocks a defender in order to get her teammate open. The screener must stand still on a screen, or else it is illegal and results in a turnover. Also referred to as "pick."

scrimmage A practice game.

set the table A player who drives toward the basket and creates an easy scoring opportunity for a teammate by drawing more defenders to herself is setting the table so that her teammate can "eat" or score easily.

shooting guard Also known as the two-guard, this player is usually a strong defender and has a good outside shot.

spin move A reverse dribble where you momentarily turn your back either left or right and swing the ball around with you.

spot-up shooter Reference to a player who is ready to shoot when she catches the ball without making a dribble move.

starters The five players who begin the game for each team.

steal When a defender takes the ball away from the offense, usually by stealing a pass or knocking away a dribble.

substitution When a player from the bench comes onto the court to play and replaces a teammate. Players can come in and out of games an unlimited number of times.

technical foul A foul assessed for one or more of the following violations: delay of game, taking too many time-outs, having too many players on the court, hanging on the rim, fighting, swearing, arguing with a referee, or being a poor sport. It results in one or two free throws and the ball out-of-bounds for the other team.

telegraph When a player looks directly at the player she is passing to, allowing the defense to read her next move and, often, steal the ball.

thirty-second clock Each team has thirty seconds from the time it throws the ball in-bounds to dribble up the court, run a play, and shoot. Each time a shot goes up, the shot clock starts over again. If the clock runs out, that is a turnover.

three-pointer A successful shot made beyond the arc, the semi-circle indicating twenty feet from the basket from all directions.

three-second violation An offensive player is only allowed in the key for three seconds at a time. She can go out and back in again, but if she is inside the key for more than three seconds that is a turnover. Also known as three in the key.

time-out A two-minute break from the action. Any player on the court can call a time-out. Each team gets three time-outs per half.

traveling When a player moves with the ball without dribbling. Also called walking.

triple-threat position When a player is in ready position with the ball she has three choices, or threats: She can pass, shoot, or dribble.

turnover When the team on offense loses possession of the ball in any other way than a missed shot. A turnover could be three seconds in the key, traveling, a steal, a shot-clock violation, or an offensive foul.

wing   An area of the court diagonally out from the block, where the guards line up to catch passes and take shots.

zone defense   The type of defense where each player guards an area on the court rather than a specific player. Typical types of zone defenses include a 2-3, or a 1-2-1 setup.

For More Information

In the United States

National Collegiate Athletic Association (NCAA)
700 West Washington Street
P.O. Box 6222
Indianapolis, IN 46206-6222
(317) 917-6222
Web site: http://www.ncaa.org

Women's National Basketball Association (WNBA)
645 Fifth Avenue
New York, NY 10022
(212) 688-9622
Web site: http://www.wnba.com

In Canada

Canada Basketball
557 Dixon Road, Suite 102
Etobicoke, ON M9W 1H7
(416) 614-8037
Web site: http://www.basketball.ca

Web Sites

Canadian Association for the
     Advancement of Women and
     Sport and Physical Activity
http://caaws.ca

Girls Basketball Resources
http://www.toprecruits.com

NCAA Basketball
http://www.ncaabasketball.net

USA Basketball
http://www.usabasketball.com

Women's Basketball Coaches Association
http://www.wbca.org

Women's Basketball Hall of Fame
http://www.wbhof.com

Online Magazines

Gball

http://www.gballmag.com

The online magazine for girls who play basketball.

Real Sports

http://www.real-sports.com

The online version of a magazine for fans and athletes involved in girls' and women's sports.

Women's Basketball

http://wbmagazine.com

This is the site for the first magazine on women's basketball.

For Further Reading

Blais, Madeleine. *In These Girls, Hope Is a Muscle.* New York: Warner Books, 1996.

Gottesman, Jane. *Game Face: What Does A Female Athlete Look Like?* New York: Random House, 2001.

Macy, Sue, and Jane Gottesman, eds. *Play Like a Girl: A Celebration of Women in Sports.* New York: Henry Holt and Co., 1999.

Rutledge, Rachel. *The Best of the Best in Basketball.* Brookfield, CT: Millbrook Press, 1998.

Weatherspoon, Teresa, Tara Sullivan, and Kelly Whiteside. *Teresa Weatherspoon's Basketball for Girls.* New York: John Wiley & Sons, 1999.

Index

About the Author

Elizabeth Gettelman is a journalist and sports equity specialist who lives in San Francisco, California. She is also active in getting girls involved in sports.

Credits

Cover, pp. 6, 9, 11, 12, 19, 20, 22, 23, 24, 27, 28, 33, 38, 45, 47, 49, 51, 53, 55 by Peter Foley; pp. 3, 5, 8, 17, 18, 35, 39, 44, 56, 59, 60 © Corbis; diagrams on pp. 4, 42–43 by Tom Forget; p. 7 © Associated Press/Ron Frehm; diagram on p. 12 by Claudia Carlson; p. 16 © Doug Pensinger/AllSport USA; p. 32 © Nathan Bilow/AllSport USA; p. 36 © Michael Krasowitz/FPG International; p. 37 © John Lawlor/FPG International; p. 41 © Superstock.

The Rosen Publishing Group would like to thank Barbara Berman and the students of John Adams Middle School, Edison, NJ.

Series Design

Danielle Goldblatt

Layout

Claudia Carlson